Stories of Welsh
2

The Prize

Siân Lewis

Illustrated by Robin Lawrie

The Prize

It was the day of this year's fair at St Mary Hill - August 26th 1892. I was up before six and had my head out of the bedroom window when my brother Levi stepped out of the house.

'Chicken!' I said.

Levi closed the front door and shook his fist at me without even looking up. Then off he went swaggering down the road with his tommy box under his arm, as if he were six feet tall. The way he was walking you'd swear he'd been a miner for as long as our dad. He hadn't. This was only his third week in Parc Slip. And he wasn't six feet tall. He was hardly taller than me and only a year older.

Will Jenkins, Dad's butty, was waiting for him two doors down.

Levi nodded at him like our dad does.

I said 'Chicken!' again under my breath.

Then they both turned the corner and I got back into the cool side of the bed, where Levi'd been.

I didn't lie there long. Nellie and Martha were soon jumping on top of me. Our other sister Kate was standing in the doorway being bossy as usual.

'Come on, Tom,' she said, 'or you'll miss the fair.'

I would never miss the August fair at St Mary Hill. It's only my brother who'd do that. Mam thought it was because he was grown-up and responsible.

'Your brother's a man now,' she said.

'But Dad's a man,' I replied. 'And he's coming to the fair. Lots of men are coming to the fair.'

It was true. Our dad had changed shift so he could take us to the fair. Levi could have changed shift too. Our dad wanted him to, but Levi was stubborn.

'It'll be the first time Levi's gone down the mine without your dad,' said Mam. 'He wants to show he can do it.'

'But he's gone with Will Jenkins,' I said back to her. 'What's the difference between going with Will or with Dad? He's still got a man looking after him.'

He was only doing it to spite me, but Mam wouldn't have that. Last year when we went to the fair Levi was bragging he'd knock a coconut off the coconut shy. For all his bragging he kept missing by a mile. Now he was scared I'd show him up. He knew I'd been practising with stones and bits of wood down by the coal yard.

Our little brother Owen was acting up that morning. Mam had a hard time spooning food into him. He got his porridge all over his face and she had to scrub him before taking him over to Nan Thomas who lives in the next street. Nan is too old to go to the fair any more, so this year she looked after Owen. Last year she'd looked after Nellie too. By the time Mam came back, half of our row was already going off to the fair.

'Lucky the sun's shining,' said Maggie next door.

'Wish it were shining on our Levi,' said Mam.

'It's his fault,' I said.

Ned Jones came clattering past just then on his bony old horse.

'Where's David?' I called to him. His son David is twelve, just like Levi.

'Gone to work, hasn't he?' said Ned, winking at me. 'Couldn't stop him. He wouldn't hear of it. I see your Levi's at work too.'

'They're keeping the mine going,' said Dad, and he and Ned laughed.

'David and our Levi are only collier boys,' I whispered to Kate. 'All Levi does is open and shut doors underground.'

Ned Jones rode off. I wished I had a horse, even a bent old thing that was only skin and bone. I wished it more and more as we walked to St Mary Hill. I could have run, but I had to keep hold of Nellie's hand and drag her along. Our dad carried her for a while, then Martha wanted to be carried, but he told her she was big enough to walk. It wasn't her first time at the fair.

You could hear the fair a mile off. It made a noise like a rusty wheel, a sort of hum filled with creaks and squeaks. The creaks and squeaks were the horses neighing, the stall holders shouting, people laughing and squealing and trying their luck. We were just one of the lines of people streaming towards it. I let go of Nellie's hand.

'Can I go on, Dad?' I said. 'Can I go on?'

'What happens when you want your lunch?' asked Mam.

'I shall be by the coconut shy, I expect. I'll only go as

far as there.'

'Go on then.'

Off I went, ducking and diving through the crowd. Some of my friends called out to me, but I didn't want to wait for them. I wanted to see how good I was after all my practising. Throwing stones at bits of wood is one thing. Coconuts is another. Some people had told me that the man on the stall glued all the coconuts down, so you couldn't ever shift them. But I knew that wasn't true. John Parry had knocked one down last year. I'd seen him. That was when I didn't have any money and when Levi wouldn't share his last three goes with me. And what did he do then? He went and wasted them all.

It wasn't much after eight o'clock in the morning. At that time people were just easing themselves around the fair, eyeing and planning and smiling. That's the best bit, when you've still got money in your pocket and you're thinking what to do with it. I was the only one in a hurry, because until I got that coconut, I wouldn't know how much money I'd have to spend.

The man on the stall was the same one as the year before. I remembered him, because he looked so rounded and polished like the brass jug on Nan Thomas's mantelpiece. He had a red, shiny face and a bushy moustache that swept over his lips. When I got there, he was brushing sawdust off his hands.

'Fancy a go, lad?' he asked in a lazy sort of way.

When I said 'Yeah,' it took him by surprise. He spruced up.

'Six balls for a ha'penny,' he said. 'Six balls for a ha'penny.'

He gathered them up and gave them to me.

I was that nervous after waiting a whole year to have a go, I made a fool of myself. I threw the balls one after the other without taking breath almost. Thunk thunk thunk thunk. They hit the sheet behind the coconuts.

'Hard luck, lad.'

I was shaking and as red as he was. I took out another ha'penny.

'Steady,' said the stall holder. 'It's early on in the day.'

'It's not early for a miner,' said a voice behind me. It was Will Jenkins's eldest son. 'His brother and my dad have been at work over two hours already and they'll be working for ten hours more, won't they, Tom?'

'Yeah,' I said.

That did it. I handed over my ha'penny and took a deep breath. I pretended I was back by the coal yard taking aim and hardly ever missing.

Thwack. My first ball hit the second coconut from the left. It didn't fall off, but it rocked. You could see it wasn't stuck down, but it was nestling very comfortably in some sawdust, so it would be hard to shift. I moved a little to the left and aimed lower. My plan was to get the ball to lift it from underneath just like a spoon lifting a whole egg from a cup.

Someone said 'Go for it, Tom,' but that was the last I heard. It was as if a wall had come down all around me and there was just me and the coconut, which gave a little

hop when the second and the third balls struck it. So the coconut wouldn't have time to properly resettle itself, I pelted the next two. Thwack Thwack.

The second of those thwacks was followed by a long delicious, floating moment. Bright bits of sawdust were flying in the air and before I knew it the coconut was topling to the ground. In my excitement I dropped the sixth ball.

'Well done, lad.' Even the stall holder was pleased. He gathered up the coconut, pushed it into my arms and boomed in my ear: 'Look, men! Look at this young lad. Can you beat that? Where are you from, lad?'

'Aberkenfig,' I said.

'Look what this young man has got to take home with him to Aberkenfig today,' the man shouted, waving his arms and making the most of it. 'How's about all the rest of you having a go? Roll up! Roll up!'

People were laughing, people were whooping and shouting and I wished our Levi was there just so I could see his face. I stuffed the coconut into my jacket pocket so hard that it ripped, then I went running off to find our mam and dad to show them what I'd done.

I'd only gone two steps when there was a low-down roaring noise, such a powerful noise that the ground shook under my feet. Thunk thunk. I looked round. Two of the coconuts had dropped off their stands. I was going to run back to see if I could claim them, when I noticed the coconut man had gone quite still. Everyone else too. Oh, there were kids squealing and horses neighing, but beneath

that was a deathly hush. People were looking in the direction of Aberkenfig.

'Why?' I said. 'What's wrong?'

No one answered.

Instead there was a wail. A man's wail. With a clatter of hoofs Ned Jones went galloping away from the fair on that bony nag of his. He headed back the way he'd come and twice as fast. Other people began running after him, helter-skelter.

Someone caught hold of my arm. It was Mam.

'Mam!' I said, pulling myself away.

'We've got to get home,' she said. 'Come on. We've got to get home, Tom.'

She ran off and I followed. By then people were crying. My sisters were waiting in a bunch by a china stall.

'Where's our dad?' I asked.

'He's gone on ahead to see what's to be done.'

'Our Levi's been blowed,' said Nellie. She was smiling. She didn't know what it meant.

I did.

'That noise,' I said to our mam, 'it wasn't Parc Slip, was it? Has there been an explosion?'

Parc Slip is not one of those pits where the miners get into a cage and drop like stones right down into the ground. You often got explosions in those pits. I'd heard our dad and his mates talk about them. In Parc Slip there's a tunnel that slopes very gently underground. I knew people got killed there sometimes, but usually only one or two. And sometimes they got injured. Maggie next door's dad was hit

by a runaway dram two years ago and hasn't been right in the head since.

'Has there been an explosion in Parc Slip?' I asked Mam again, but Mam had no breath to answer me, so then I knew it was true.

Horses were galloping past us, traps rattling, and there was such a scuffling, a panting and a gasping, as if all the noise of the fair had got snarled up, like sometimes when old rusty wires get caught in the wheels of carts. The coconut was bumping against my hip bone and I would have thrown it away, only I thought if Levi had had to come home early because of the explosion, I could show it to him anyway. So I let it bump, bump, bump, and there was a sore patch on my hip bone when I got home.

Our Levi wasn't there. Nan Thomas was standing on our doorstep with Owen in her arms. Owen was covered in blackberry juice, so he looked like a little tiny collier boy, but that wasn't the first thing I noticed. The first thing I noticed was tears dripping off Nan Thomas's face. She said to our mam, 'I'll look after them' and our mam pushed my sisters into the house. She would have pushed me too, only I pulled away fast.

We went running down the street towards the pit. There were other people gathered round there. Sarah Jenkins, Will's wife, looked round. When she saw it was Mam and me, she shook her head.

'What?' gasped Mam, taking terrible fright, so that Sarah had to hold her hand to steady her.

'We don't know anything yet,' she said. 'The rescue

party went down a while ago. Your Ben's gone too.'

There were bobbies standing round the entrance to the mine, so we couldn't go near, but any minute I expected to see our dad come out, bringing Levi and all the rest with him. It's not that far underground, not half as far as the St Mary Hill fair and we'd had plenty of time to come back from that.

Some men were arriving from neighbouring pits to help with the rescue. I was watching them, when I felt someone tug at my arm. It was my friend Danny. He made signs for me to follow him. We went round the back of the crowd and he showed me a horse lying dead on the ground. It was Ned Jones's horse. Ned had ridden him so fast that the bony old thing had dropped dead just as they got to the pit head.

All that fast riding didn't do him any good either. Mam told me that night that David, Ned's son, had been found dead. By then I'd seen other bodies brought out. It was gas that had killed them. Mam said that maybe, if Levi was lucky, he might be sitting in a little hole where the gas hadn't got to.

Wesley Rees's dad was lucky. He got away safe from the pit. Most men didn't. Even James Bowen, who'd tried to rescue them, didn't get out alive. After six days several miners were still missing and our dad still hadn't found Levi. Dad explained that you couldn't go fast. You had to dig carefully through rock falls and watch out for gas. You took down a canary in a cage and if it fell ill, it meant you had to pump

fresh air in. Most of the time Dad was too tired to say anything. When he got home, Mam would rush to get the tin bath out, put food on the table and then he'd fall on his bed in a sound sleep, before going back to the pit to start all over again.

We didn't go out to play that week. Mam said it wasn't respectful. Kate and I understood. Martha did too, but she sometimes forgot. Nellie and Owen didn't understand at all.

One day, when Dad was asleep, Mam sent me upstairs to stop Nellie making a row. She was playing in the bedroom I shared with Levi. I thought she had Owen with her, because she was saying, 'Good baby. 'Cause you're a good little baby, I'll tie your hair up for you. Shall I tie your hair up?'

When I went in, she was sitting on the floor by our bed. But she didn't have Owen with her. What she had was a coconut wrapped in an old vest.

'Where d'you get that?' I burst out.

'Sh!' said Nellie. She wasn't worried about our dad. She just didn't want me to disturb the coconut. I dropped my voice anyway.

'Where d'you get that?' I whispered, because I'd forgotten all about that coconut.

Nellie didn't answer and there was no point in asking her again. I let her play with it. When I went to bed that night, I found the coconut lying on the floor and I took it to bed with me just to pretend I had company. Levi says it's that dark in the pit, it's like being blind, if you didn't have

your lamp, that is, and your lamp doesn't give much light. Levi's lamp would have gone off by now and soon it would be seven days that he'd spent in that dark hole.

I was glad when morning came.

That morning they were burying nine men in the churchyard. Mam wouldn't let us peep, but we could hear the singing. We had to keep quiet. It had been a quiet couple of days. People didn't gather round the pit head any more. Anyone who was waiting for news just stayed at home. Kate was black-leading the fender, Martha was feeding Owen, Nellie was playing and I was out the back digging up potatoes when we heard a commotion.

We'd heard such commotions before. The last was when they found the bodies of John Harris and a couple of others. There'd been shouts, sharp cries that sounded like a flock of crows rising into the air. Whenever there was a commotion, Mam would stop whatever she was doing and press her hands to her face.

The commotion reached the end of our row. Even though they were still singing in Nebo, doors were opening and people shouting. I heard someone shout Mam's name:

'Rachel Ann! Rachel Ann!'

That was when I dropped the potatoes and ran into the house. Mam had already got the front door open. I caught a glimpse of Dad's face. Dad stumbled past her. In his arms he had a bundle wrapped in a blanket. There were faces crowding in the doorway. They watched him lay the bundle on our table.

Mam cried out.

Dad had unwrapped the blanket and there was our Levi. His eyes were wide open and his face was covered in a mash of coal dust, the sort of mash you get when it rains. Mam cried out again and threw her arms round him.

Nellie tugged at my sleeve. She was smiling up at me. 'Is our Levi died?' she asked.

I didn't know, even though I could hear noises in the blanket Mam was holding. They were noises like an animal whimpering.

'Ma-am,' began Nellie.

She didn't get a chance to finish, because Mam turned round and said, 'Get out the back now, there's good children. Off you go now.'

'I want to know if Levi's dead,' I said stubbornly.

'Course he's not!' said Mam, but her eyes started to spout tears. The dust from Levi had rubbed off onto her face and the tears made trickles through it.

'Get out the back now,' Dad roared.

So we all went except Owen, who was sitting on the floor by the front door, so we couldn't grab him.

Through the back window we saw Dad give Levi a sip of water that made him cough. Mam was filling the tub. She and Dad together undressed Levi, sat him in the tub and washed him all over very slowly and carefully. Owen was trying to help. He was squealing and patting Levi on the head and Levi didn't once yell at him to go away.

Levi wasn't saying a word. Once I saw him stare at me as if he didn't know who I was.

Nellie had climbed on a bucket and pressed her face to the window.

'Is our Levi an angel?' she asked.

'No,' said Martha.

'She means ghost,' said Kate.

'Is he?' asked Nellie.

No one answered her until Nan Thomas came. She said, 'No, he's not a ghost. He's had a shock, poor dab. All that time in the darkness. He'll be fine, I should think.'

Will Jenkins was fine already. I'd heard his voice in the street. Dad had gone to thank him for looking after our Levi. Will Jenkins had made Levi sit still with him and three other men till the rescuers came. They'd been trapped by a rock fall and if they'd dug themselves out, most likely they would have been killed by the gas on the other side.

We had to keep quiet that afternoon, even quieter than when Levi was lost. When we were having our tea, Mam had to feed him. He kept on staring as if he were stupid. There was no noise in the house except for Owen laughing and squawking. We were glad when Dad carried Levi up to bed out of our way.

Mam sat with him all that evening until it was time for me to go to bed. I said I didn't mind sleeping on the floor downstairs. I didn't want to sleep next to him. I didn't think I could keep quiet, I told Mam, but Mam wouldn't listen to me.

I tiptoed up. The curtains were open and I could see Levi was lying on his side of the bed with his back to me. I thought he was asleep. I wanted him to stay asleep. I got undressed quietly and crawled up my side of the bed, instead of leaping over him. Half way up I saw that his eyes were open.

They were wide open and staring at something on the bed. They were staring at that old coconut.

'It's all right,' I said. 'I didn't win it.'

Levi said nothing.

'It fell off the stand when the ground shook,' I said. 'It was that explosion of yours that did it.'

After a pause the bed creaked and I heard my brother's voice say, 'I knew you wouldn't do it.'

'You were right,' I said.

Then I jumped in beside him.